Bible
Promises
for
Forgiveness

A Tyndale nonfiction imprint

Bible Promises for Forgiveness

> Forgive as the Lord forgave you. COLOSSIANS 3:13

Micah E. Davis

Visit Tyndale online at tyndale.com.

Visit Tyndale Momentum online at tyndalemomentum.com.

Visit the author at micahedavis.com.

Tyndale, Tyndale's quill logo, *Tyndale Momentum*, and the Tyndale Momentum logo are registered trademarks of Tyndale House Ministries. Tyndale Momentum is a nonfiction imprint of Tyndale House Publishers, Carol Stream, Illinois.

Bible Promises for Forgiveness

Copyright © 2025 by Micah Davis. All rights reserved.

Cover photograph of abstract canvas copyright © Laurin Rinder/Adobe Stock. All rights reserved.

Cover design by Dean H. Renninger and Libby Dykstra

Interior design by Laura Cruise

Edited by Claire Lloyd

Published in association with the literary agency of The Steve Laube Agency.

Unless otherwise indicated, all Scripture quotations are taken from the *Holy Bible*, New Living Translation, copyright © 1996, 2004, 2015 by Tyndale House Foundation. Used by permission of Tyndale House Publishers, Carol Stream, Illinois 60188. All rights reserved.

The verse on the cover is taken from the Holy Bible, *New International Version,*® NIV.® Copyright © 1973, 1978, 1984, 2011 by Biblica, Inc.® Used by permission. All rights reserved worldwide.

Scripture quotations marked ESV are from The ESV® Bible (The Holy Bible, English Standard Version®), copyright © 2001 by Crossway, a publishing ministry of Good News Publishers. Used by permission. All rights reserved.

Scripture quotations marked NIV are taken from the Holy Bible, *New International Version,*® NIV.® Copyright © 1973, 1978, 1984, 2011 by Biblica, Inc.® Used by permission. All rights reserved worldwide.

The URLs in this book were verified prior to publication. The publisher is not responsible for content in the links, links that have expired, or websites that have changed ownership after that time.

For information about special discounts for bulk purchases, please contact Tyndale House Publishers at csresponse@tyndale.com, or call 1-855-277-9400.

ISBN 979-8-4005-0650-5

Printed in the United States of America

31	30	29	28	27	26	25
7	6	5	4	3	2	1

Introduction

To be honest, I wish a resource like this didn't have to be written.

I wish the world were functioning as it was intended to. I wish that relational harmony were present between all and that there was unity, peace, joy, hope, and love among the nations. I wish that forgiveness were a way of life that we practiced perfectly every time.

But unfortunately, that is not the case.

Our world is broken. Sin has infected every nitty-gritty corner of our society. And relational strife is at the heart of dissonance between who we are and who we were created to be.

How do we mend what life seems to break? Ultimately, it is only through the grace Jesus demonstrates and invites us to extend. Thus, it is necessary to reflect on the biblical imperative of forgiveness, know what Scripture says about it, and then put these principles into practice.

Ah . . . forgiveness. What *is* forgiveness? Essentially, to forgive is

1. to pardon;
2. to excuse someone from having to pay a debt they owe you.[1]

For millennia, the term has been misused and misunderstood. Quite frankly, many of us have had it up to *here* with the idea of Christian forgiveness. We've witnessed manipulation, hurt, and hypocrisy justified under the guise of "forgiveness." We've seen people silenced into "moving on," "letting go," and "forgetting." Others have been let off the hook—scot-free—in the name of forgiveness. Some, when called out publicly for their actions, misuse Scripture to justify those actions.

These examples and more are enough to make our blood boil and heart race. *EXACTLY! That's EXACTLY why forgiveness doesn't work.*

Still, deep down, we desire to forgive and be forgiven. I'm sure we can all recollect moments when we've been exposed for the hurt we've caused and needed forgiveness. It's never fun. Even less fun are the moments when we've been hurt and have hoped that the other person asking for forgiveness would bring healing—only for accountability to be entirely absent, avoided, or dismissed.

Might I add that I have often stood at the front of this line.

In my life up to this point, I have watched father figure after father figure and pastor after pastor fail. And I'm not talking about internet celebrity pastors. I'm talking about close, personal mentors who were entrusted with guarding and guiding my (and thousands of others') spiritual journey.

In fact, as I'm writing this sentence, another article has dropped revealing that the pastor of the church that founded my high school (a formative leader in my own life and walk with Jesus over the years) has just had his resignation accepted by his congregation for what's been deemed to be a bullying and intimidating leadership style.

Sigh.

I've experienced some of the worst pain imaginable. I've felt hurt, betrayed, and abandoned. I've been lied to. I've been dismissed. I've been wounded beyond measure.

And yet . . .

I have witnessed God—the great Healer—show up time after time.

In the moments when I've desperately wanted to choose cynicism, I've instead fought hard to cultivate compassion. In the moments when I've longed for revenge, I've prayed for justice and mercy to win out. In the moments when I've felt betrayed, I've found refuge in a God who sees me.[2] In the moments when I've witnessed the world equate failure with finality, I've experienced—firsthand—a God who redeems our failure for his glory.

My friend, the pages ahead do not come from a distant, disembodied laboratory. I have not labored to concoct the perfect formula for experiencing and administering forgiveness. Instead, I lived it—in all its earthy mess, pain, and imperfection.

But through the difficulties of forgiveness, I have discovered something good, true, and beautiful. A beam of light in a dark, dark world. The reality is that relational conflict can be a fire that causes devastating burns all around. Or . . . it can be a fire of refinement.

Truthfully, that's the trickiest aspect of forgiveness. There's no formula, simply a fire. It's messy, it's uncomfortable, and it's almost never linear. The journey we are embarking on will be one of two steps forward and three steps back. You will have good days and hard days. Please hear me: that's okay.

I want you to know—first and foremost—that you are seen and loved by a God who knows you. But friends, I have to be honest: we can't follow Jesus and *avoid* pressing further into the concept of forgiveness.

But you don't understand.
You can't possibly know what they've done.
What they've done is unforgivable.

I don't disagree with you. However, Jesus does: "If you forgive those who sin against you, your heavenly Father will forgive you. But if you refuse to forgive others, your Father will not forgive your sins."[3]

That's a clear causal statement. If, then. Within Jesus' two-sentence imperative on forgiveness are four necessary acts:

1. Our need to forgive others.
2. Our need to be forgiven by others.
3. Our need to forgive ourselves.
4. Our need to forgive God.

That is the journey we are invited to go on. A journey to redeem our past from the clutches of hurt and pain. A journey to be restored into an integrated, peaceful, reconciling person, living fully in the love of God. And a journey to seek reconciliation in light of the new creation to come.

The good news is that this journey need not be taken alone. In fact, you and I are far from the first to step onto this path. In the coming days, I hope that you will discover the rich library of wisdom that the writers of the Scriptures have to offer us. I hope that you will be empowered to ask for and extend biblical forgiveness.

From Jonah to Joseph, Paul to Peter, the prevailing theme of the Bible is one of forgiveness, reconciliation, and redemption. On the other side of forgiveness is freedom. The freedom that you've been desperately longing for. It's possible to receive, but it comes at a cost. And it's a price—as you'll soon see—worth paying every single time.

Forgiving Others

Forgiving someone is both a practice and a process. It is a conscious decision we make. It is something we actively do. Forgiveness as a practice is acknowledging a debt that is owed and making the determination to wipe the ledger clean. But oftentimes, there's a process to forgiving others as well. Why?

Because to forgive someone means that they have hurt us in some way. And enduring hurt is never a simplistic, black-and-white matter. This is what makes forgiveness difficult and why a process is necessary. Some days are easier—other days we revert to responding out of hurt rather than healing. However, over time, when we follow the process, forgiveness is possible and brings freedom.

The first step is to grieve and acknowledge the injustice that has been done. Whether small or big, we have to face the hurt that we feel has been directed toward us. To miss this crucial step allows denial to creep in. And when denial creeps in, we are unable to see clearly. The sooner we can acknowledge the hurt that's been done, face it, and grieve it, the sooner we can begin to heal.

After we grieve, we must reassess and take inventory of what comes next. Are there new boundaries that must be drawn with the person who hurt you? Are there natural consequences that need to be communicated to them, either by you or a trusted third party? Are there practices that need to be put in place for your protection moving forward? This is a crucial part of the healing process. Setting up boundaries allows you to heal at your own pace. This is healthy and helpful, so long as you're pressing into the third piece of this process, which is to build.

At some point, the relationship that has been deconstructed can and should be reconstructed into whatever its next iteration is going to be. Jesus longs for us to rebuild toward wholeness, restoration, and reconciliation.

Now, I know this is not always possible. Rebuilding doesn't mean that trust will ever be fully earned back. But it does mean that we love and live with a desire and hopefulness that it can.

Whatever hurt you are bringing with you today, know that Jesus sees you. And he longs to heal your hurt and bring restoration. Jesus' own process of enduring betrayal, slander, and torment ended with forgiveness.[1] He showed us the way forward and gave us hope that reconciliation can take place. This was the heart of Jesus' mission on earth. Out of his love and mercy, he came to reconcile himself to a people who had disowned, disrespected, and distanced themselves from him.

Jesus' pledge of forgiveness reminds us of the beauty of the mercy we first received and are now entrusted to extend. However, his promise of restoration—of making all wrongs right—reminds us that justice is in tow. God will not be mocked. Evil will not prevail.

The apostle James says it this way: "Speak and act as those who are going to be judged by the law that gives freedom, because judgment without mercy will be shown to anyone who has not been merciful. Mercy triumphs over judgment."[2]

We follow the way of our Rabbi. We lead with mercy but love with justice.

When you have been hurt by someone

The LORD is close to the brokenhearted;
he rescues those whose spirits are crushed.

PSALM 34:18

[Jesus] was despised and rejected—
a man of sorrows, acquainted with deepest
grief.

ISAIAH 53:3

God blesses those who mourn,
for they will be comforted.

MATTHEW 5:4

God is our merciful Father and the source of
all comfort.

2 CORINTHIANS 1:3

When a situation feels unfair

I have spent the majority of this year reading and rereading Peter's first letter to exiles throughout the ancient world. And I have been struck by Jesus' response in the face of intense persecution. Peter writes, "He did not retaliate when he was insulted, nor threaten revenge when he suffered. He left his case in the hands of God, who always judges fairly."[3]

Recently, I was publicly criticized. I felt that the criticism was unfair, unfounded, and lacked a great deal of context. The author's conclusions seemed vague and spiteful. I sensed jealousy in the attack. Everything in me wanted to email this person and set the record straight. But Peter's words turned up in my mind over and over again: "He did not retaliate when he was insulted." I decided that no reply was the most gracious reply.

Jesus knows what it's like to be accused and mistreated. He understands.

I take Peter's words to mean that Jesus most likely endured the real, raw, human emotions that we often process. Insults and suffering most likely left him feeling vulnerable, exposed, insecure, frustrated, angry. But notice where he directed those emotions: "He left his case in the hands of God, who always judges fairly."

What a beautiful example Jesus sets. It's not that we can't feel hurt when someone hurls insults at us. It's that we are to avoid compounding evil with evil. Instead, we break the cycle by redirecting any desire for revenge or retribution into the hands of God. In God's hands, our hurts can be properly held. In our hands, hurt often fuels further hurt.

Let the one with scars on his hands hold the weight of sin you've incurred. Those scars demonstrate that he's done it before and can do it again.

> God is my shield,
> saving those whose hearts are true
> and right.
> God is an honest judge.
>
> PSALM 7:10-11

For the LORD loves justice,
	and he will never abandon the godly.
PSALM 37:28

The LORD lifts up those who are weighed
down.
PSALM 146:8

God blesses those who hunger and thirst for
justice, for they will be satisfied.
MATTHEW 5:6

Remember that the heavenly Father to whom
you pray has no favorites. He will judge or
reward you according to what you do.
1 PETER 1:17

To this you were called, because Christ
suffered for you, leaving you an example,
that you should follow in his steps.

"He committed no sin,
	and no deceit was found in his mouth."

When they hurled their insults at him, he
did not retaliate; when he suffered, he made
no threats. Instead, he entrusted himself to
him who judges justly.
1 PETER 2:21-23, NIV

When you feel angry

People with understanding control their anger;
a hot temper shows great foolishness.

PROVERBS 14:29

Don't sin by letting anger control you.

EPHESIANS 4:26

Understand this, my dear brothers and
sisters: You must all be quick to listen, slow
to speak, and slow to get angry. Human
anger does not produce the righteousness
God desires.

JAMES 1:19-20

When you aren't sure why you should forgive

A peaceful heart leads to a healthy body.

PROVERBS 14:30

If you forgive those who sin against you,
your heavenly Father will forgive you. But if
you refuse to forgive others, your Father will
not forgive your sins.

MATTHEW 6:14-15

Make allowance for each other's faults, and
forgive anyone who offends you. Remember,

the Lord forgave you, so you must forgive
others.

COLOSSIANS 3:13

You were cleansed from your sins when you
obeyed the truth, so now you must show
sincere love to each other as brothers and
sisters. Love each other deeply with all your
heart.

1 PETER 1:22

There will be no mercy for those who have
not shown mercy to others. But if you have
been merciful, God will be merciful when he
judges you.

JAMES 2:13

We love each other because he loved us first.

1 JOHN 4:19

The Parable of the Unforgiving Servant

The Kingdom of Heaven can be compared
to a king who decided to bring his accounts
up to date with servants who had borrowed
money from him. In the process, one of
his debtors was brought in who owed him
millions of dollars. He couldn't pay, so his
master ordered that he be sold—along with

his wife, his children, and everything he owned—to pay the debt.

But the man fell down before his master and begged him, "Please, be patient with me, and I will pay it all." Then his master was filled with pity for him, and he released him and forgave his debt.

But when the man left the king, he went to a fellow servant who owed him a few thousand dollars. He grabbed him by the throat and demanded instant payment.

His fellow servant fell down before him and begged for a little more time. "Be patient with me, and I will pay it," he pleaded. But his creditor wouldn't wait. He had the man arrested and put in prison until the debt could be paid in full.

When some of the other servants saw this, they were very upset. They went to the king and told him everything that had happened. Then the king called in the man he had forgiven and said, "You evil servant! I forgave you that tremendous debt because you pleaded with me. Shouldn't you have mercy on your fellow servant, just as I had mercy on you?" Then the angry king sent

the man to prison to be tortured until he
had paid his entire debt.

That's what my heavenly Father will do
to you if you refuse to forgive your brothers
and sisters from your heart.

MATTHEW 18:23-35

"Then his master was filled with pity for him, and he released him and forgave his debt." That phrase—"forgave his debt"—is, in Greek, the word *aphiēmi*, which literally means to release or surrender a debt.[4]

This story in Matthew 18 is a wild, lavish show of grace on the part of the king. But the feel-good story doesn't last long.

Upon leaving, the servant goes and finds another servant who owes him one hundred silver coins. The Scriptures call these *denarii*, and the sum (roughly one hundred days' worth of wages) is much less valuable than the debt the servant originally owed the king.[5] This fellow servant pleads with the servant in the same way the servant pleaded with the king to have mercy on him. But instead, the servant throws him into prison until he can repay the debt.[6]

Others see this take place and—sensing the extreme injustice of it all—take their disapproval to the king. The king—now enraged—throws this servant into jail to be tortured until his unpayable debt can be paid back (i.e., for eternity).

In case the point isn't clear: Forgive and you will be forgiven. Don't forgive and you won't be forgiven. Sounds straightforward, but we're all aware of how difficult this is, right? Forgiving is counterintuitive to everything we feel as human beings, and it's certainly countercultural to the world we live in today.

What most of our society fails to realize is that by withholding what we are meant to give, we miss out on receiving the very thing we need. And it comes at a cost either way.

To forgive costs us greatly. I'm not—in any way—attempting to diminish this. Forgiveness comes at a cost for the offended, the disinherited, and the left out. In extending forgiveness, we are absorbing a loss (a debt). It is—fundamentally—an imbalanced equation. The person asking for forgiveness receives a net gain while the person who credits forgiveness receives a net loss. There is sacrifice involved. The act of forgiveness is embracing such sacrifice without demanding anything in return.

However, to *not* forgive might end up costing us more. Do you know anyone with a deep-seated bitterness and resentment who has lived as a person marked by joy, peace, kindness, and love? I don't.

Forgiveness flies in the face of all things rational, coherent, and equal. It's fundamentally unequal, irrational, and incoherent. It's lavish. It's merciful. It's abundant. It's necessary in experiencing what Jesus calls life and life to the full.

When you don't believe you can ever forgive

Don't be afraid, for I am with you.
    Don't be discouraged, for I am your God.
I will strengthen you and help you.

ISAIAH 41:10

I am about to do something new.
    See, I have already begun! Do you not
        see it?
I will make a pathway through the wilderness.
    I will create rivers in the dry wasteland.

ISAIAH 43:19

Don't copy the behavior and customs of this world, but let God transform you into a new person by changing the way you think.

ROMANS 12:2

I can do everything through Christ, who gives me strength.

PHILIPPIANS 4:13

When you have bitter and resentful thoughts

Bitterness, when not dealt with, can be deadly.

We all know at least one person who has faced hardship and become unkind, angry, or spiteful. Bitterness tends to harden us over time. It's much more subtle than explosive. It's easy to become bitter when we feel we have been wronged.

If we're not careful, we can routinely give bitterness and resentfulness a foothold in our hearts. Every time we do not let go, the grip on our soul gets tighter and tighter. But if this is your story, there is still hope!

My friend, an invitation is offered to you and me to cut off the roots of bitterness, cynicism, and anger that are festering within and to release those who have hurt us. This does not excuse them from being held accountable to right and just consequences for their actions. However, what forgiveness *does* do is disintegrate the bitterness that often callouses our hearts. It transforms the root system of our family trees, offering opportunities for generational sin to be no more.

In place of hurt comes healing. In place of a destructive past and frustrating present comes a liberating future where we freely forgive.

> Do not judge others, and you will not be
> judged. For you will be treated as you treat

others. The standard you use in judging is the standard by which you will be judged.

MATTHEW 7:1-2

Don't let evil conquer you, but conquer evil by doing good.

ROMANS 12:21

Fix your thoughts on what is true, and honorable, and right, and pure, and lovely, and admirable. Think about things that are excellent and worthy of praise.

PHILIPPIANS 4:8

Watch out that no poisonous root of bitterness grows up to trouble you, corrupting many.

HEBREWS 12:15

When the person who harmed you never apologized or admitted their wrong

God will judge us for everything we do, including every secret thing, whether good or bad.

ECCLESIASTES 12:14

Each of us will give a personal account to God.

ROMANS 14:12

Let us run with endurance the race God has set before us. We do this by keeping our eyes on Jesus, the champion who initiates and perfects our faith. Because of the joy awaiting him, he endured the cross, disregarding its shame. Now he is seated in the place of honor beside God's throne. Think of all the hostility he endured from sinful people; then you won't become weary and give up.

HEBREWS 12:1-3

If you are suffering in a manner that pleases God, keep on doing what is right, and trust your lives to the God who created you, for he will never fail you.

1 PETER 4:19

Jesus Forgives Those Who Crucified Him

Jesus said, "Father, forgive them, for they don't know what they are doing."

LUKE 23:34

Forgiveness is not vindictive.
Forgiveness is costly. It cost Jesus everything. And yet, even in the midst of betrayal, public shaming, and a humiliating execution, Jesus had the audacity to cry,

"Father, forgive them, for they don't know what they are doing."

Forgiveness does not seek retribution or revenge under the guise of justice. This is where we're beginning to see a shift. Rather than holding those in power accountable, victimhood has become a vehicle of vengeance. While I'm all for healthy reform, outrage in the name of accountability is tearing apart the fabric of our society. Instead of seeking to extend mercy and hear opposing views—politically, socially, religiously, or spiritually—we can be tempted to either shout one another down or silence each other out.

It was Dr. Martin Luther King Jr. who once said, "Forgiveness means reconciliation, a coming together again."[7]

We have moved far away from this as we've replaced the God of the Bible with the god of self at the center of our lives. If our highest concern is always what's best for ourselves rather than what's best for all of us, we'll never recover a true ethos of forgiveness.

We must learn to hold justice and mercy, compassion and conviction, truth and grace in a tension that allows for costly grace to infiltrate our relationships.

When you keep ruminating on a hurtful experience

Commit everything you do to the Lord.
　　Trust him, and he will help you.
He will make your innocence radiate like the dawn,
　　and the justice of your cause will shine like
　　　　the noonday sun.

Be still in the presence of the Lord,
　　and wait patiently for him to act.
Don't worry about evil people who prosper
　　or fret about their wicked schemes.

Stop being angry!
　　Turn from your rage!
Do not lose your temper—
　　it only leads to harm.

PSALM 37:5-8

Why am I discouraged?
　　Why is my heart so sad?
I will put my hope in God!
　　I will praise him again—
　　my Savior and my God!

PSALM 43:5

Love prospers when a fault is forgiven,
　　but dwelling on it separates close friends.

PROVERBS 17:9

I am leaving you with a gift—peace of mind and heart. And the peace I give is a gift the world cannot give. So don't be troubled or afraid.

JOHN 14:27

Don't worry about anything; instead, pray about everything. Tell God what you need, and thank him for all he has done. Then you will experience God's peace, which exceeds anything we can understand. His peace will guard your hearts and minds as you live in Christ Jesus.

PHILIPPIANS 4:6-7

When those who do harm seem to prosper

Don't worry about the wicked
    or envy those who do wrong.
For like grass, they soon fade away.
    Like spring flowers, they soon wither.

PSALM 37:1-2

Don't be misled—you cannot mock the justice of God. You will always harvest what you plant.

GALATIANS 6:7

When you are worried that the harm done to you will be forgotten if you forgive

In Matthew 5, Jesus teaches, "If you are offering your gift at the altar and there remember that your brother or sister has something against you, leave your gift there in front of the altar. First go and be reconciled to them; then come and offer your gift."[8] He is saying, "Look, if you're going to worship me, if you're going to follow me, then you must learn to *forgive*."

Not forget. Not turn a blind eye. Not excuse. *Forgive.*

Jesus has credibility to say these words. This is a man who was abused, beaten, spit on, physically attacked, publicly shamed, relationally abandoned, and deeply hurt. And yet, to those very people, Jesus says, "Father, forgive them, for they do not know what they are doing."[9]

Your hurt is real. So was Jesus'. But there is a thread here that can be traced through the New Testament. Unforgiveness only prolongs and spreads hurt. Jesus is explicit about requiring the consistent pursuit of forgiveness and reconciliation.

This type of rhetoric may seem genuinely foreign to us nowadays. Or perhaps it even seems outright offensive. The focus in our modern moment is often less about reconciliation and more about getting even.

But—in your most honest assessment—has getting even ever truly healed the pain within? Have you ever pursued revenge and then gone to sleep at night with the lasting thought, *That was the right thing to do*? Never.

In my experience, the longer I hold on to bitterness, the more the wounds I have incurred become infected. There is certainly a time to leave the hurt alone and not ruminate or immediately fix it, and we *need* time to heal, but time alone does not heal our wounds. At some point, we must be willing to do the work of repair—for no one's sake more than our own.

Failing to forgive past offenses hurts no one more than ourselves. And Jesus knows this. He understands how much *more* it matters for us to start the process of healing even if we didn't start the process that led to hurt. He knows that forgiveness may not change the other person's heart, motives, or future direction. However, true, authentic forgiveness always changes our heart, motives, and future direction. And it is out of this posture that we discover the scandal of grace to its fullest extent.

> You keep track of all my sorrows.
> You have collected all my tears in your
> bottle.

You have recorded each one in your book.

PSALM 56:8

God watches how people live;
he sees everything they do.

JOB 34:21-22

Give all your worries and cares to God, for
he cares about you.

1 PETER 5:7

When you desire to repay hurt for hurt

Don't say, "I will get even for this wrong."
Wait for the LORD to handle the matter.

PROVERBS 20:22

Fools vent their anger,
but the wise quietly hold it back.

PROVERBS 29:11

To you who are willing to listen, I say, love
your enemies! Do good to those who hate
you. Bless those who curse you. Pray for
those who hurt you.

LUKE 6:27-28

Never pay back evil with more evil.

ROMANS 12:17

When you are tempted to hold a grudge

Sensible people control their temper;
they earn respect by overlooking wrongs.

PROVERBS 19:11

[Love] keeps no record of being wronged.

1 CORINTHIANS 13:5

Most important of all, continue to show
deep love for each other, for love covers a
multitude of sins.

1 PETER 4:8

When you are working to empathize with someone who has wronged you

The other day I found myself watching one of *those* Netflix documentaries. You know? The one about the famous person who had a tragic public meltdown and is now being exploited for millions of dollars to further crucify their character in front of the masses?

Is that a bit cynical? Perhaps. But when we take an honest look at our own hearts, we have to admit that there's a tendency to be both disgusted and invigorated by the failure of others. *What a creep. I would NEVER do something like that*, I found myself thinking as I watched the documentary. There's a part of human nature that feeds off failure. We deny, dismiss, and hide our own shortcomings while seeking content that highlights the failings of others.

We are all one decision away from being in a position we never imagined we ever would be. Poor choices happen gradually over time, when we drift and drift and drift before . . . BAM! A split-second decision pushes us off the ledge into failure. But make no mistake, we'd been walking toward that ledge for quite some time.

My point is, we all have our warts, limitations, and struggles. Paul labeled it a "thorn in [the] flesh."[10] At its best, this "thorn in [the] flesh" is the constant (albeit uncomfortable) reminder that we are not perfect. We all sin and fall short of the glory of God.[11]

This reality helps us to develop empathy for others. It does not dismiss or excuse someone when they fall short, but it does remind us that our response should be one that we'd like to receive when (not if) we find ourselves in a similar situation at some point: forgiveness.

We often overestimate our spiritual maturity. None of us are as far as we think. I say that with humility. I am first and foremost included in that statement. But it's better to be aware of our blindness than to be ignorant that it even exists.

Lord, have mercy on us all.

Do to others whatever you would like them
to do to you.

MATTHEW 7:12

Get rid of all bitterness, rage, anger, harsh
words, and slander, as well as all types of
evil behavior. Instead, be kind to each other,
tenderhearted, forgiving one another, just as
God through Christ has forgiven you.

EPHESIANS 4:31-32

Share each other's burdens, and in this way
obey the law of Christ. If you think you are
too important to help someone, you are only
fooling yourself. You are not that important.

GALATIANS 6:2-3

All of you should be of one mind.
Sympathize with each other. Love each other
as brothers and sisters.

1 PETER 3:8

**When you struggle to desire good for someone who
has harmed you**

You must be compassionate, just as your
Father is compassionate.

LUKE 6:36

Bless those who persecute you. Don't curse them; pray that God will bless them.

ROMANS 12:14

Put on your new nature, and be renewed as you learn to know your Creator and become like him.

COLOSSIANS 3:10

When you fear being hurt again

"The body keeps the score," wrote Bessel van der Kolk.[12] Not only does relational hurt affect our physical bodies in the present, but it has been known to show up genealogically. The pain that is embedded into us can often be passed down to future generations. We see this often in broken homes and the effects this can have on one's children and even children's children.

The stress response in the brain negatively affects the body as it is flooded with chemicals intended to destroy what it perceives as a threat. Over time, these chemicals can actually fight against the healthy cells in our body, leading to chronic illness, sleep deprivation, and debilitating depression, among other things.[13]

These responses are ways God is able to get our attention—physically—that something wrong has happened. It is important to pay attention to these responses, especially when they occur around someone else. To forgive someone does not mean we must subject ourselves to their presence.

Not only is confusing forgiveness with immediate reconciliation unhealthy, but often it can be harmful—for instance, citing Matthew 18:15-17 should not be an excuse for maintaining an unsafe relationship.

Until a person has repented, desires reconciliation, and demonstrates true, actionable progress toward said reconciliation, they shouldn't be entrusted with restored relationship. This is not only accountability for the perpetrator, but also protection for the wronged.

We can trust God to take care of us and love those who hurt us while being wise in how we interact with those people going forward.

> The Lord is my shepherd;
>   I have all that I need.
> He lets me rest in green meadows;
>   he leads me beside peaceful streams.
>   He renews my strength.
> He guides me along right paths,
>   bringing honor to his name.
> Even when I walk
>   through the darkest valley,
> I will not be afraid,
>   for you are close beside me.

Your rod and your staff
    protect and comfort me.
You prepare a feast for me
    in the presence of my enemies.
You honor me by anointing my head with oil.
    My cup overflows with blessings.
Surely your goodness and unfailing love will
        pursue me
    all the days of my life,
and I will live in the house of the LORD
    forever.

PSALM 23:1-6

The LORD is my light and my salvation—
    so why should I be afraid?
The LORD is my fortress, protecting me from
        danger,
    so why should I tremble?

PSALM 27:1

Love your enemies! Do good to them. Lend
to them without expecting to be repaid.
Then your reward from heaven will be very
great, and you will truly be acting as children
of the Most High, for he is kind to those
who are unthankful and wicked.

LUKE 6:35

God has not given us a spirit of fear
and timidity, but of power, love, and
self-discipline.

2 TIMOTHY 1:7

Paul Calls the Corinthian Church to Forgive

Forgive whatever needs to be forgiven . . . so
that Satan will not outsmart us. For we are
familiar with his evil schemes.

2 CORINTHIANS 2:10-11

In 1 Corinthians 5, we see Paul handling a case of local church discipline. A man is sleeping with his father's wife. Paul calls for the Corinthians to discipline church members whose actions compromise the holiness of the community. However, the Corinthians are passive in their accountability. Paul writes this letter to wake them up to their duty as brothers and sisters in Christ.

In 2 Corinthians 2, it seems the Corinthians have listened. They've expelled this man from their assembly in an effort to force him to choose between continuing to live in sin or repenting. Evidently he repents, but now the Corinthians have swung the opposite way. Even though he has repented, the Corinthian church will not restore this man into fellowship. Now *they* are the ones living in sin. So, Paul urges this church to "reaffirm [their] love for him."[14]

In Paul's eyes, this matter is just as urgent as the original matter. Failing to restore this man into fellowship after repentance opened the door for Satan to create division within the broader community. Satan could potentially deploy his "evil schemes" among them.

To withhold forgiveness is to play right into Satan's hands in our relationships. Resentment, pride, anger, etc. drive a wedge between us, destroying intimacy and fueling distrust. We must work diligently to maintain harmony in our relationships. That can only be done when we restore those who repent.

When someone who hurt you asks for forgiveness

> Peter came to him and asked, "Lord, how often should I forgive someone who sins against me? Seven times?"
>
> "No, not seven times," Jesus replied, "but seventy times seven!
>
> MATTHEW 18:21-22

> If there is repentance, forgive. Even if that person wrongs you seven times a day and each time turns again and asks forgiveness, you must forgive.
>
> LUKE 17:3-4

God blesses those who are merciful, for they
will be shown mercy.

MATTHEW 5:7

Asking for Forgiveness

In order to authentically receive forgiveness, you must be genuinely sorry for what you've done or who you've hurt. Forgiveness may be extended to you despite an absence of remorse, but you can't receive it unless you genuinely apologize. We must feel the magnitude and weight of our sin. This is a good thing. God does not bring us face-to-face with our sin to shame or condemn us. Rather, he shows us our sin to reveal how powerless and not in control we are. How desperately we need his grace.

If you feel true remorse, then in order to receive forgiveness, you must commit to recourse. You must choose a new way of life. In the Scriptures, this is referred to as repentance.

In Greek, to repent is the word *metanoeō*, and it means to turn around or to go another direction.[1] Receiving forgiveness from someone we've hurt, wounded, or upset should motivate us to change. If not, we are not loving our neighbor as ourselves. Instead, we are selfishly manipulating a system for our advantage. And the cycle of hurt will only be prolonged.

Humility is at the heart of forgiveness. Understand that humility counteracts shame. Humility reflects; shame deflects. Humility invites; shame expels. Humility opens; shame closes.

We forgive because we are forgiven. We receive undeserved forgiveness from others because God gave each of us undeserved forgiveness himself.

To repent—to turn around—is actionable. Recourse means taking responsibility for the ways we've fallen short and intentionally choosing to live differently.

When we fall short, consequences are often given to us for our corrective benefit. This is the side of God that we do not want to talk about. A God of grace and mercy seems too loving to bring about judgment on anyone, right? But "God cannot be mocked" and "[He] cannot tolerate wrongdoing."[2] So, like a good parent, he uses consequences to correct and discipline his children—not to punish us but to redirect us into becoming the inheritors of his Kingdom he has promised we will be.

Authentic remorse leads to recourse—to repentance. This is good news, my friends. God does not bring us to repentance out of spite, in anger, or even in retribution. Rather, it is God's kindness that leads us to repentance.[3]

No matter whether the person you've hurt chooses to forgive you or not, we all must get to a place where we understand that, as sons and daughters of God, we are *forgiven*.

Forgiveness's power is not dependent on *feeling* forgiven. When we seek God, we find forgiveness.[4]

There is no doubt that this is a war we all find ourselves in. The church fathers and mothers often referred to it as a war against the three enemies of the soul: the world, the flesh, and the devil.[5] Each is seeking to devour us in doubt and confuse us with half-truths or outright lies. So, Satan will do everything he can to convince you:

"You aren't forgiven."

"No one will forget."

"Your life is over."

"There's no second chance."

"You blew it."

"That's just who you are."

But we must fight tooth and nail to press into who God says we are. In Christ, we are forgiven. God wants to use you, every part of you—your flaws, failures, fears, doubts, strengths, gifts, talents, and abilities—to change this world as we know it. To help bring heaven on earth.

If you find yourself in need of forgiveness, know that we serve a God who says, **three strikes, you're . . . forgiven.**

When you wonder if you should ask someone for forgiveness

> People who conceal their sins will not prosper,
>> but if they confess and turn from them, they
>>> will receive mercy.

PROVERBS 28:13

> Remember, it is sin to know what you ought
> to do and then not do it.

JAMES 4:17

When you struggle to admit your mistakes

> Pride leads to disgrace,
>> but with humility comes wisdom.

PROVERBS 11:2

> In repentance and rest is your salvation,
>> in quietness and trust is your strength.

ISAIAH 30:15, NIV

There is more joy in heaven over one lost
sinner who repents and returns to God than
over ninety-nine others who are righteous
and haven't strayed away!

LUKE 15:7

A Prayer for Forgiveness

From the time of his youth, David was set apart.

Yes, he was young. Yes, he was stubborn and
snarky. But he was *good*. In Hebrew, he was *tov*. And
the tov within him propelled David from shepherd,
to warrior, to commander, to king. All along the way,
throughout the entirety of this ascension, David was
tov, he was good. His acts were good, his words were
good, his relationships were good, his treatment of
others—toward those he loved, and more impor-
tantly, toward those who hated him—was good.

But then, a single moment changes the narrative
of David's life. From his palace roof he sees a naked
woman named Bathsheba, requests for her to come
to the palace, learns that she's married to one of his
soldiers, disregards that fact, sleeps with her, and
impregnates her.[6]

In fear of being found out, David then has
Bathsheba's husband, Uriah, brought home. David
wines and dines Uriah multiple times, hoping that

he'll go home to his wife so the whole event will be covered up (remember, there's no DNA testing to prove what really occurred).[7] But David's plan doesn't work, so he sends Uriah to the front lines of the war being fought for Israel—a war being fought, in some part, *for* King David himself—and he instructs the general of his army, Joab, to command everyone to abandon Uriah there to die, which they do.

David then takes Bathsheba—Uriah's wife—as his own.[8]

The consequences of David's sin are enormous. The child Bathsheba bears dies shortly after.

Down the line, further sexual assault (of his daughter by his son), incest, murder, and an attempted insurrection on David's throne can all be traced back to *this* decision.

Eventually, his life and reign begins to crash and burn all around him. It's a tragic story of a good man and family giving in to a depth of sin and depravity previously incomprehensible.

And yet, the Scriptures routinely refer to David as "faithful" and "a man after God's heart." How can this be? Because despite David's shortcomings, David confessed his sin and—in a state of brokenness and repentance—came home. Psalm 51:1-12 is the key prayer that David offers to God as he remorsefully apologizes for his wrong actions. And guess what?

God forgives him. God is always faithful to forgive us when we ask.

Have mercy on me, O God,
    because of your unfailing love.
Because of your great compassion,
    blot out the stain of my sins.
Wash me clean from my guilt.
    Purify me from my sin.
For I recognize my rebellion;
    it haunts me day and night.
Against you, and you alone, have I sinned;
    I have done what is evil in your sight.
You will be proved right in what you say,
    and your judgment against me is just.
For I was born a sinner—
    yes, from the moment my mother conceived
        me.
But you desire honesty from the womb,
    teaching me wisdom even there.
Purify me from my sins, and I will be clean;
    wash me, and I will be whiter than snow.
Oh, give me back my joy again;
    you have broken me—
    now let me rejoice.
Don't keep looking at my sins.
    Remove the stain of my guilt.

Create in me a clean heart, O God.
> Renew a loyal spirit within me.
Do not banish me from your presence,
> and don't take your Holy Spirit from me.
Restore to me the joy of your salvation,
> and make me willing to obey you.

When you realize that repentance requires changed actions

Produce fruit in keeping with repentance.

MATTHEW 3:8, NIV

Put on your new nature, created to be like God—truly righteous and holy.

EPHESIANS 4:24

Put to death the sinful, earthly things lurking within you. Have nothing to do with sexual immorality, impurity, lust, and evil desires.

COLOSSIANS 3:5

Dear children, let's not merely say that we love each other; let us show the truth by our actions.

1 JOHN 3:18

Jesus Encounters the Woman Caught in Adultery

As [Jesus] was speaking, the teachers of religious law and the Pharisees brought a woman who had been caught in the act of adultery. They put her in front of the crowd.

"Teacher," they said to Jesus, "this woman was caught in the act of adultery. The law of Moses says to stone her. What do you say?"

They were trying to trap him into saying something they could use against him, but Jesus stooped down and wrote in the dust with his finger. They kept demanding an answer, so he stood up again and said, "All right, but let the one who has never sinned throw the first stone!" Then he stooped down again and wrote in the dust.

When the accusers heard this, they slipped away one by one, beginning with the oldest, until only Jesus was left in the middle of the crowd with the woman. Then Jesus stood up again and said to the woman, "Where are your accusers? Didn't even one of them condemn you?"

"No, Lord," she said.

> And Jesus said, "Neither do I. Go and sin no more."
>
> JOHN 8:3-11

So, a group of religious leaders—called the Pharisees—bring a woman caught in adultery to Jesus. A few questions should arise: First, how was this woman caught engaging in such a private and intimate act? Also, where was the man caught in adultery? Foul play is surely to be suspected.

"They made her stand before the group and said to Jesus, 'Teacher, this woman was caught in the act of adultery.'"[9] This phrase, "made her stand," is a literal translation of the Greek verb *histémi*.[10] It implies *force*.

Now, we must keep in mind that Jesus is teaching publicly in the most iconic place in all of Jerusalem: the Temple. In other words, these Pharisees are not interested in justice; they're interested in creating a spectacle. This is a WWE match, mixed with an episode of Jerry Springer, being live streamed, all on steroids.

The intent is clear: ruthless humiliation. They're seeking to send a message.

Eventually, Jesus stands up and says, "Let the one who has never sinned throw the first stone."

One by one, the Pharisees—starting with the oldest—drop their stones and walk away.

In this moment, only Jesus and the woman are left.

At this, he directly acknowledges the woman for the first time and asks where her accusers are and if anyone has condemned her. Her response? No one.

This is the moment.

In this woman's time of greatest pain, she is set free. No longer is she bound by shame; instead, she is released into life to the full through the forgiveness of her sins. She is chosen, redeemed, and accepted by her Lord and Savior. Out of this new identity, a new invitation is given: "Go and sin no more."

Jesus never *agrees* with or *approves* of the woman's choices. But he does *accept* her as a daughter of the Most High.

We can lovingly disapprove of another's actions without assassinating their character. It is in the gracious home of love that many prodigals feel compelled to return. Mercy, mercy, mercy, with justice in tow.

When someone rejects your apology and refuses to extend forgiveness

The LORD is watching everywhere,
    keeping his eye on both the evil and the good.

PROVERBS 15:3

We are each responsible for our own conduct.

GALATIANS 6:5

When you feel trapped in a sinful pattern

Search for the LORD and for his strength;
continually seek him.

1 CHRONICLES 16:11

The temptations in your life are no different
from what others experience. And God is
faithful. He will not allow the temptation to
be more than you can stand. When you are
tempted, he will show you a way out so that
you can endure.

1 CORINTHIANS 10:13

Let the Holy Spirit guide your lives. Then
you won't be doing what your sinful nature
craves.

GALATIANS 5:16

[Jesus] gave his life to free us from every
kind of sin, to cleanse us, and to make us his
very own people, totally committed to doing
good deeds.

TITUS 2:14

Humble yourselves before God. Resist the
devil, and he will flee from you. Come close
to God, and God will come close to you.
Wash your hands, you sinners; purify your

hearts, for your loyalty is divided between God and the world.

JAMES 4:7-8

When you enter a reconciliation process

We will speak the truth in love, growing in every way more and more like Christ, who is the head of his body, the church.

EPHESIANS 4:15

Above all, clothe yourselves with love, which binds us all together in perfect harmony. And let the peace that comes from Christ rule in your hearts. For as members of one body you are called to live in peace. And always be thankful.

COLOSSIANS 3:14-15

When a reconciliation process feels slow and difficult

God blesses those who work for peace, for they will be called the children of God.

MATTHEW 5:9

Let's not get tired of doing what is good. At just the right time we will reap a harvest of blessing if we don't give up.

GALATIANS 6:9

Jacob and Esau Reconcile

> Esau ran to meet him and embraced him,
> threw his arms around his neck, and kissed
> him. And they both wept.
>
> GENESIS 33:4

One day, Jacob sees his brother, Esau, whom—decades earlier—he had betrayed, approaching with a company of four hundred men. Jacob walks ahead of his family and bows to the ground seven times. A sign of immense respect.

You have to wonder what is going through Jacob's mind while he bows, right? Is he waiting for Esau to come running, screaming, waving a sword to chop his brother's head off? Will Esau shoot an arrow through his heart while his eyes are to the ground? Will the four hundred men begin to encircle him?

Actually, none of that happens.

Instead, "Esau ran to meet him and embraced him; threw his arms around his neck, and kissed him. And they both wept."[11]

Stunning.

Rather than seeking revenge, Esau seeks reconciliation. This is a forgiveness that can't be bought.

This decision literally had generational effects.

Years later, Joseph's experience of suffering and God's kindness in the midst of it allowed him to differentiate between humanity's brokenness and God's goodness. Rather than blaming God for the terrible things that had happened to him, he was able to see God's kindness through the difficulties of life and forgive those who had wounded him.

But how? How did he learn to forgive such unforgettable offenses?

He watched his uncle do it. Check out this oft-looked-over verse in Genesis 33: "[Jacob] put the female servants and their children in front, Leah and her children next, and Rachel and Joseph in the rear. He himself went on ahead and bowed down to the ground seven times as he approached his brother."[12]

That's right. Joseph was in the rear of Jacob's camp as his father bowed to the ground seven times waiting to see how his uncle—who'd had everything stripped away from him by his brother—would respond. And it was a response of kindness, of forgiveness, of debt-release.

When you desire to build back someone's trust

Kind words are like honey—
    sweet to the soul and healthy for the body.
PROVERBS 16:24

This is my commandment: Love each other
in the same way I have loved you.

JOHN 15:12

Don't be selfish; don't try to impress others.
Be humble, thinking of others as better than
yourselves. Don't look out only for your own
interests, but take an interest in others, too.

PHILIPPIANS 2:3-4

**When you wonder if you should confess communal
sin that you have witnessed or participated in**

At last my people will confess their sins and
the sins of their ancestors. . . . Then I will
remember my covenant with Jacob and my
covenant with Isaac and my covenant with
Abraham, and I will remember the land.

LEVITICUS 26:40, 42

If my people who are called by my name will
humble themselves and pray and seek my
face and turn from their wicked ways, I will
hear from heaven and will forgive their sins
and restore their land.

2 CHRONICLES 7:14

Nehemiah and the Israelites Practice Corporate Confession and Repentance

> Those of Israelite descent separated
> themselves from all foreigners as they
> confessed their own sins and the sins of their
> ancestors. They remained standing in place
> for three hours while the Book of the Law of
> the LORD their God was read aloud to them.
> Then for three more hours they confessed
> their sins and worshiped the LORD their God.
>
> NEHEMIAH 9:2-3

If there is one element of corporate worship that we have almost completely lost (at least in my nondenominational, Protestant tradition), it is communal confession.

We may lament when tragedy strikes, but in terms of our sin we rarely own what there is to own as a body. If there is injustice, racism, disobedience, pride, greed, etc. in my own heart, then surely it is in the heart of my parishioners. I would guess it'd be the same for you, your pastors, and your church.

And yet, we rarely acknowledge such darkness within and around us.

This is a tragedy.

All throughout the Scriptures, we witness God's people being called—collectively—to repent. Israel's prophets and leaders—be it Ezra, Nehemiah, Daniel—routinely call God's people to corporate confession in an effort to ask for God's forgiveness. This plea is followed by a pledge to turn around, go a different direction, and live a different way.

While we may not have the authority to change this in our churches, we certainly have opportunities to implement corporate confession into the daily and weekly rhythms of our lives. We can confess with our family, friends, small group, Bible study, coworkers, and neighbors. It takes a leader who is willing to be vulnerable first and has the courage to invite others to join them.

Let us be a people who recover the sacred act of communal confession.

When repentance brings freedom from sin

> Because you belong to him, the power of
> the life-giving Spirit has freed you from the
> power of sin that leads to death.
> ROMANS 8:2

> The kind of sorrow God wants us to
> experience leads us away from sin and results

in salvation. There's no regret for that kind
of sorrow.

2 CORINTHIANS 7:10

Throw off your old sinful nature and your
former way of life, which is corrupted by lust
and deception. Instead, let the Spirit renew
your thoughts and attitudes. Put on your
new nature, created to be like God—truly
righteous and holy.

EPHESIANS 4:22-24

When repentance brings healing

Oh, what joy for those
    whose disobedience is forgiven,
    whose sin is put out of sight!
Yes, what joy for those
    whose record the LORD has cleared of guilt,
    whose lives are lived in complete honesty!

PSALM 32:1-2

Now repent of your sins and turn to God,
so that your sins may be wiped away. Then
times of refreshment will come from the
presence of the Lord.

ACTS 3:19-20

Confess your sins to each other and pray
for each other so that you may be healed.
The earnest prayer of a righteous person
has great power and produces wonderful
results.

JAMES 5:16

When repentance brings restoration

Look at those who are honest and good,
    for a wonderful future awaits those who love
        peace.

PSALM 37:37

He will give a crown of beauty for ashes,
a joyous blessing instead of mourning,
    festive praise instead of despair.
In their righteousness, they will be like great
        oaks
    that the LORD has planted for his own glory.

ISAIAH 61:3

In his kindness God called you to share in
his eternal glory by means of Christ Jesus. So
after you have suffered a little while, he will
restore, support, and strengthen you, and he
will place you on a firm foundation.

1 PETER 5:10

Forgiving Yourself

My friends, our God is a God who flips the script over and over and over again. He's beckoning you to shed your shame and to step into the future he has for you.

Remember, forgiveness is a practice. It's a conscious decision. A decision we have to make routinely, even for ourselves. We must choose to leave our sin, put it to death, and go another way. To return home, into the loving, warm embrace of our Father's forgiving arms.

Many of us fall into the trap of subconsciously believing that God only loves us because Jesus died for us. Right? We might think, *God has to forgive me because I put my faith and trust in Jesus. He doesn't actually want to.*

This is what so many of us who struggle to forgive ourselves believe. We see God the Father as this ruler of the cosmos who's separate, jaded, and upset with humanity because we can never get it right or figure it out. Thank goodness for Jesus, because if it weren't for Jesus, God would hate us.

In fact, perhaps you're reading this today and you think that God does hate you. You're grateful for Jesus' sacrifice that's saved you, but you've yet to place your faith and trust in a God who loves you. Does this resonate with you?

Here's the deal: we can forgive ourselves because God forgives us. God does not love us because Jesus died for us; Jesus died for us because God loves us. Such a subtle shift, but one that will change your perspective forever.

Read John 3:16 through *that* lens! "For God so loved the world . . ." (NIV).

He—God—so loved the world that he gave (or he sent, or he offered) his one and only Son, that whoever believes in him shall not perish but have eternal life.

Our God is a God who holds the ultimate trump card, the ace in the hole. It's his Son, Jesus. God turned an instrument of pain into a pillar of new life. God turned death itself on its head and fashioned resurrected life. This is the gospel. Good News for all who repent and believe.

The apostle John wrote, "If we confess our sins, he is faithful and just and will forgive us our sins and purify us from all unrighteousness."[1]

He is faithful and just to forgive.

God loves you. God forgives you. Often these truths are half-heartedly said, and the weight and power of these words is lost. But don't miss this.

God *loves* you.

God *forgives* you.

Now, the invitation before you and me is to forgive ourselves. To make a conscious decision to trust his character, to offer ourselves in submission to his love, mercy, and grace, and to walk intentionally in step with the God who sees, knows, and loves you just as you are.

When you need to forgive yourself

In order to get out from underneath the grip of self-hate and regret, we have to make a choice, a decision. First, to see God for who he really is. What you believe about God determines everything.

What comes into your mind when you think about God? Is he the God of John 3:16—the God who loves you unconditionally and with reckless abandon? Is he a God who pursues you over and over again—even when you reject him, even when you curse him, even when you deny him?

My friend, God is after you. Not in a gotcha, you're caught, shame-ridden way, but in a way that beckons and yearns for you to come out of hiding. In the loving arms of a Savior, and in the presence of brothers and sisters in the faith, you are safe.

He's there. He loves you. He sees you.

For many of us, we see God as the forgiver with conditions. We think that if we don't meet his standards, then he won't forgive us. Others of us see God as our earthly father (and that's a painful comparison), or perhaps we see God as someone who betrayed us or whose approval we could never win. Maybe your view of God is hurting your ability to not only forgive others—but to forgive yourself.

We have to make a decision to see God for who he really is. But then we also must make a decision to see ourselves as we really are, in Christ.

Dig into the Scriptures. Read God's Word. Talk to him—ask him to reveal his true self to you and to reveal your true self to you. Make your own list of who he says you are. Let his truth wash over you and remind you that you are . . .

a conqueror (Romans 12:21)
chosen (Matthew 22:14)
valued (1 Peter 1:18)
loved (John 15:9)
redeemed (Psalm 107:2)
cared for (Psalm 112:7)
disciplined (Proverbs 3:11)
able to endure (James 1:3; Romans 5:3-4)

And then make the decision to believe in his character. To trust that he is who he says he is. And that *you* are who he says you are.

> The LORD is like a father to his children,
>> tender and compassionate to those who fear
>> him.
> For he knows how weak we are;
>> he remembers we are only dust.

PSALM 103:13-14

Jesus said, "Come to me, all of you who are weary and carry heavy burdens, and I will give you rest. Take my yoke upon you. Let me teach you, because I am humble and gentle at heart, and you will find rest for your souls."

MATTHEW 11:28-29

Therefore, there is now no condemnation for those who are in Christ Jesus.

ROMANS 8:1, NIV

You were cleansed; you were made holy; you were made right with God by calling on the name of the Lord Jesus Christ and by the Spirit of our God.

1 CORINTHIANS 6:11

Forgetting the past and looking forward to
what lies ahead, I press on to reach the end
of the race and receive the heavenly prize
for which God, through Christ Jesus, is
calling us.

PHILIPPIANS 3:13-14

When you feel like a failure

Unless we're able to grasp the inevitable reality of living in a broken, fallen world, full of broken, fallen people who will let us down and fail us just as we let them down and fail them, we'll never be able to run the race of forgiveness.

Rather than running toward forgiveness, we'll run toward bitterness to protect ourselves from further pain. Or we'll run toward addiction to numb our emotions. Or we'll run toward revenge so that if we can't finish the race, no one else can either.

There's a reason we have to stay in our own lane in a track race. It's so we don't trip up or accidentally hurt anyone else. The Way, the Truth, and the Life that is Jesus Christ is the boundary of our lane. It is through his teachings that we're able to understand and come to terms with our inevitable starting point, run our race freely and cleanly, and finish at the end with a forgiving—not a bitter, cynical, or resentful—heart.

The race is ready to be run. The question is, Are

you ready and willing to begin? The starting point is failure. And that's actually the best place possible to take off from.

I see failure as a catalytic reminder of my sinful nature. Failure shows up daily (often multiple times per day) in my life. I can't avoid it. As Paul says, "I do not understand what I do. For what I want to do I do not do, but what I hate I do."[2] Failure is a constant struggle that each of us must be willing to embrace.

Now, I'm not talking about an embrace, pursuit, or ambition of *moral* failure. It should never be our aim to cheat on our spouse, lie on our taxes, or steal from our business. However, I am talking about an embrace of the *reality* of failure.

Failure is inevitable. It's embedded into my life and yours. From the time we are born, we fail. And from the time we are born, we learn from failure.

From learning to walk, to riding a bike, to earning a degree, failing is part of living. The choice before us is whether we will trust in a God who works through and in spite of our failure or if we'll settle for the lie that our failure defines us.

> My health may fail, and my spirit may grow weak,
> but God remains the strength of my heart;
> he is mine forever.

PSALM 73:26

I cried out, "I am slipping!"
>   but your unfailing love, O LORD, supported
>   me.
When doubts filled my mind,
>   your comfort gave me renewed hope and
>   cheer.

PSALM 94:18-19

Oh, what a miserable person I am! Who will free me from this life that is dominated by sin and death? Thank God! The answer is in Jesus Christ our Lord.

ROMANS 7:24-25

Each time he said, "My grace is all you need. My power works best in weakness." So now I am glad to boast about my weaknesses, so that the power of Christ can work through me. That's why I take pleasure in my weaknesses, and in the insults, hardships, persecutions, and troubles that I suffer for Christ. For when I am weak, then I am strong.

2 CORINTHIANS 12:9-10

When you feel guilty for harming someone

Turn away from evil and do good.
>   Search for peace, and work to maintain it.

PSALM 34:14

If you are presenting a sacrifice at the altar
in the Temple and you suddenly remember
that someone has something against you,
leave your sacrifice there at the altar. Go and
be reconciled to that person. Then come and
offer your sacrifice to God.

MATTHEW 5:23-24

When you feel burdened by your own sin

When I refused to confess my sin,
>   my body wasted away,
>   and I groaned all day long.
Day and night your hand of discipline was heavy
>   on me.
>   My strength evaporated like water in the
>   summer heat.

Finally, I confessed all my sins to you
>   and stopped trying to hide my guilt.
I said to myself, "I will confess my rebellion to
>   the LORD."
>   And you forgave me! All my guilt is gone.

PSALM 32:3-5

Jesus answered them, "Healthy people
don't need a doctor—sick people do. I have
come to call not those who think they are

righteous, but those who know they are
sinners and need to repent."

LUKE 5:31-32

Let there be tears for what you have done.
Let there be sorrow and deep grief. Let there
be sadness instead of laughter, and gloom
instead of joy. Humble yourselves before the
Lord, and he will lift you up in honor.

JAMES 4:9-10

Joseph Forgives His Brothers

They sent this message to Joseph: "Before
your father died, he instructed us to say
to you: 'Please forgive your brothers for
the great wrong they did to you—for their
sin in treating you so cruelly.' So we, the
servants of the God of your father, beg
you to forgive our sin." When Joseph
received the message, he broke down and
wept. Then his brothers came and threw
themselves down before Joseph. "Look, we
are your slaves!" they said.

But Joseph replied, "Don't be afraid of
me. Am I God, that I can punish you? You
intended to harm me, but God intended it
all for good. He brought me to this position

so I could save the lives of many people. No, don't be afraid. I will continue to take care of you and your children."

GENESIS 50:16-21

Fascinating, isn't it?

Joseph's brothers are so fearful of Joseph that they manufacture a death wish that Jacob supposedly had left for Joseph.

But notice Joseph's response to his brothers: "Joseph wept."

Why did he weep?

I believe Joseph wept because after all he had endured, after all he had suffered, and after all he had fought through to reconcile with his brothers who had betrayed him, they had the audacity to essentially say, "So, is this reconciliation for real? Or were you just faking it until Dad was gone? Because if so, please don't kill us."

At face value, that seems to be enough to make Joseph weep. But I think Joseph's tears run deeper than disappointment.

I wonder if in this moment, Joseph's first instinct is to weep because he's frustrated. Because he's deeply hurt that his brothers have not accepted—much less believe—his undeserved offer of forgiveness. Perhaps Joseph—through his tears—is communicating, "How could you not believe I forgive you? After everything I've done? How do you think this isn't real?"

This is the tragedy of unforgiveness. When we've been forgiven but have failed to forgive ourselves, not only does it hurt us, but it spits in the face of the gracious offer that's been extended to us.

Instead of seeing Joseph for who he really was, they cowered in fear, desperate to cling to any sense of control they felt they still had. Instead of seeing God as a God of forgiveness, we cower in fear, believing punishment, shame, and rebuke are the only things heading our way.

This doesn't have to be your story. Friend, forgiven people forgive people. Joseph was able to extend only what he had first received. And he wanted his brothers to experience that too.

Our God is a God of forgiveness. You can't give what you don't possess. So let Jesus meet you in the mess of your life. Revenge is not yours to take. It is yours to surrender. Offer what you have received, and let God work out the rest.

When you wonder if God still loves you

> O Lord, you are so good, so ready to forgive,
>   so full of unfailing love for all who ask for
>   your help.

PSALM 86:5

This is how God loved the world: He gave his one and only Son, so that everyone who believes in him will not perish but have eternal life. God sent his Son into the world not to judge the world, but to save the world through him.

JOHN 3:16-17

God showed his great love for us by sending Christ to die for us while we were still sinners.

ROMANS 5:8

When you feel ashamed even after repenting and receiving forgiveness

Who dares accuse us whom God has chosen for his own? No one—for God himself has given us right standing with himself. Who then will condemn us? No one—for Christ Jesus died for us and was raised to life for us, and he is sitting in the place of honor at God's right hand, pleading for us.

ROMANS 8:33-34

This is how we know that we belong to the truth and how we set our hearts at rest in his presence: If our hearts condemn us, we know that God is greater than our hearts, and he knows everything.

1 JOHN 3:19-20, NIV

When you are looking for rhythms that will turn your heart toward forgiveness

There are two practices we can regularly partake in that remind us of the forgiving nature of Christ: communion (the Eucharist) and prayer (particularly the Lord's Prayer).

Communion reminds us of the supreme sacrifice Christ offered and the new covenant that's been made available to us through the shedding of his blood. As we regularly gather around the table in the presence of brothers and sisters, we are afforded the opportunity to confess our sins, ask for and receive forgiveness from one another, and reflect on the reconciliation made possible through Christ's atoning sacrifice.

Within the Lord's Prayer is a line that—if prayed daily (as our church does)—consistently reminds us of our need to receive and extend forgiveness. That line says, "Forgive us our sins, for we also forgive everyone who sins against us." This is a prayer of reconciliation. Reconciliation was a major theme for Jesus. Often it went hand in hand with prayer. Why? Because reconciliation is about restoration. It's about something broken being made whole. And unforgiveness, bitterness, and resentment keep us from experiencing life to the full.

So, do not see the picture of forgiveness in this line from the Lord's Prayer as a box to check. Rather, see it as a burden to lay down.

Forgiveness hands the cup of judgment and justice back to the only one who can rightly handle it—Jesus. In his hands, we trust that all will be made right. And so, we—full of faith—pardon others, believing that God will—as Jesus promises—pardon us.

Forgiveness becomes a healing ointment for our souls to be restored into right relationship with God and with our neighbor. To Jesus, it's critical. For us, it should be as well. Regularly, we are to reflect on how Jesus' sacrifice on the cross bought us forgiveness in the first place. Daily, we are to pray in a posture of forgiveness.

As we partake in these practices, we are routinely training ourselves to become more and more forgiving.

> As they were eating, Jesus took some bread
> and blessed it. Then he broke it in pieces and
> gave it to the disciples, saying, "Take this
> and eat it, for this is my body."
> And he took a cup of wine and gave
> thanks to God for it. He gave it to them and
> said, "Each of you drink from it, for this

is my blood, which confirms the covenant between God and his people. It is poured out as a sacrifice to forgive the sins of many."

MATTHEW 26:26-28

Jesus said, "This is how you should pray: 'Father, may your name be kept holy. May your Kingdom come soon. Give us each day the food we need, and forgive us our sins, as we forgive those who sin against us. And don't let us yield to temptation.'"

LUKE 11:2-4

Jesus Reinstates Peter

After breakfast Jesus asked Simon Peter, "Simon son of John, do you love me more than these?"

"Yes, Lord," Peter replied, "you know I love you."

"Then feed my lambs," Jesus told him.

Jesus repeated the question: "Simon son of John, do you love me?"

"Yes, Lord," Peter said, "you know I love you."

"Then take care of my sheep," Jesus said.

A third time he asked him, "Simon son of John, do you love me?"

> Peter was hurt that Jesus asked the question a third time. He said, "Lord, you know everything. You know that I love you."
>
> Jesus said, "Then feed my sheep."
>
> JOHN 21:15-17

The number three has great significance in Peter's life. Throughout the Gospels, Peter falls asleep three times, Peter denies Jesus three times. Jesus hangs on a cross in darkness for three hours. Jesus lies in a tomb dead for three days. And then Jesus resurrects, conquering death, sin, and failure forever.

In the first recorded conversation post-resurrection between Jesus and his disciples, he says a singular statement three times: "Peace be with you!"[3] In the first recorded conversation post-resurrection between Peter and Jesus, he asks Peter a simple question *three* times.

Notice that Peter was hurt after Jesus asked him the third time. Why? Because Peter was still operating by the standard Jewish law of his day. If someone asks you something three times, you've reached the limit. Three questions, he's out. Point blank. Period.

But Jesus was rewriting the script.

For every abandonment, every denial, every failure that Peter had committed . . . forgiveness was waiting for him.

The New International Version translation heads this passage with the title "Jesus Reinstates Peter," because that's exactly what is happening. Peter the denier, liar, and abandoner steps fully into the redeemed namesake Jesus gives him. The rock on which Jesus will build his church.

"Then [Jesus] said to him, 'Follow me!'"[4]

Wouldn't you know, this is one of the last recorded lines to Peter in the Gospels. A new story is being written. One that picks up in Acts 2 when Peter addresses the crowd with the first sermon after Pentecost. Full of the Holy Spirit, Peter the rock goes on to build Christ's church.

As it turns out, failure isn't final. Forgiveness is.

Three strikes . . . you're forgiven.

Forgiving God

What comes to mind when you think of God?

Is he the spitting image of the faulty earthly father you grew up with? Is he distant, uninviting, or impatient? A put-off God with his arms crossed and foot tapping? Is he overly loving and indulgent? An easygoing God who wants you to feel good all the time? Perhaps God is impersonal to you. He's a being, a mystical force, a pie in the sky that you neither know nor believe knows you.

A. W. Tozer once wrote, "What comes into our minds when we think about God is the most important thing about us."[1] So, again, I ask you: What comes to mind when you think of God?

In Exodus 34, God reintroduces himself and his character in full force to Moses. He says, "The Lord, the Lord, the compassionate and gracious God, slow to anger, abounding in love and faithfulness, maintaining love to thousands, and forgiving wickedness, rebellion and sin. Yet he does not leave the guilty unpunished; he punishes the children and their children for the sin of the parents to the third and fourth generation."[2]

Now, there is much to unpack in that description. But for our intents and purposes, notice the characteristics that God leads with in describing himself: Compassionate and gracious. Slow to anger. Abounding in love and faithfulness.

In the Hebrew Scriptures, order matters. Order clues us in on what is most important. God leading with the fact that he is compassionate and gracious tells us something about the essence of his nature. He is a God of forgiveness.

God sees you—just as you are, with all your brokenness, all your pain, all your insecurities, all your secrets and sins—and he *loves* you. He wants what's best for you. He's looking out for you. He's with you. His love abounds for you.

This is an important foundation to lay as we continue this journey of forgiveness. Right-sizing God the Father as a Father whose love for you is infinite, unchanging, and everlasting is paramount.

The apostle John writes that "we love because he first loved us."[3] We are an image of God. Our very existence was made in his likeness. Our job is to mirror back to God what he shows us.

Therefore, we forgive because he first forgave us. "For God so loved the world that he gave his one and only Son, that whoever believes in him shall not perish but have eternal life. For God did not send his Son into the world to condemn the world, but to save the world through him."[4]

Eternal life is freely given to us, not just into eternity but here and now. And part of the inbreaking of heaven on earth is reconciling what has been broken and healing what has been hurt.

Forgiveness is a gospel issue. Forgiveness has been extended and entrusted to us to carry out. Because we have experienced grace for our mistakes, shortcomings, and sins, we offer grace to others who make mistakes, fall short, and sin.

This isn't easy, but it is necessary. Because genuine transformation does not express itself in selfish preservation but in selfless offering. God is not asking us to do anything he himself was not willing to do.

Together, we will discover not just the necessity but the beauty of forgiveness. A forgiveness that we first receive before we are ever asked to offer it.

When you need assurance that justice will be done

The LORD reigns forever,
> executing judgment from his throne.

He will judge the world with justice
    and rule the nations with fairness.
PSALM 9:7-8

God says, "At the time I have planned,
    I will bring justice against the wicked."
PSALM 75:2

The LORD gives righteousness
    and justice to all who are treated unfairly.
PSALM 103:6

God shows his anger from heaven against all
sinful, wicked people who suppress the truth
by their wickedness.
ROMANS 1:18

A day of anger is coming, when God's
righteous judgment will be revealed. He
will judge everyone according to what they
have done. He will give eternal life to those
who keep on doing good, seeking after the
glory and honor and immortality that God
offers. But he will pour out his anger and
wrath on those who live for themselves, who
refuse to obey the truth and instead live
lives of wickedness. There will be trouble
and calamity for everyone who keeps on
doing what is evil—for the Jew first and

also for the Gentile. But there will be glory and honor and peace from God for all who do good—for the Jew first and also for the Gentile. For God does not show favoritism.

ROMANS 2:5-11

Dear friends, never take revenge. Leave that to the righteous anger of God. For the Scriptures say, "I will take revenge; I will pay them back," says the LORD.

ROMANS 12:19

When unforgiveness negatively affects your relationship with God

When you are praying, first forgive anyone you are holding a grudge against, so that your Father in heaven will forgive your sins, too.

MARK 11:25

Do not judge others, and you will not be judged. Do not condemn others, or it will all come back against you. Forgive others, and you will be forgiven.

LUKE 6:37

If someone says, "I love God," but hates a fellow believer, that person is a liar; for if we don't love people we can see, how can we love God, whom we cannot see? And he has given us this command: Those who love God must also love their fellow believers.

1 JOHN 4:20-21

When you need to be reminded that we are all capable of harming others

Why worry about a speck in your friend's eye when you have a log in your own? How can you think of saying to your friend, "Let me help you get rid of that speck in your eye," when you can't see past the log in your own eye? Hypocrite! First get rid of the log in your own eye; then you will see well enough to deal with the speck in your friend's eye.

MATTHEW 7:3-5

You may think you can condemn such people, but you are just as bad, and you have no excuse! When you say they are wicked and should be punished, you are condemning yourself, for you who judge others do these very same things.

ROMANS 2:1

No one is righteous—not even one.

ROMANS 3:10

The person who keeps all of the laws except
one is as guilty as a person who has broken
all of God's laws.

JAMES 2:10

**When you need to be reminded that God honors
a repentant heart**

The sacrifice you desire is a broken spirit.
    You will not reject a broken and repentant
        heart, O God.

PSALM 51:17

My hands have made both heaven and earth;
    they and everything in them are mine.
    I, the LORD, have spoken!
I will bless those who have humble and contrite
        hearts,
    who tremble at my word.

ISAIAH 66:2

Those whom I love I rebuke and discipline.
So be earnest and repent.

REVELATION 3:19, NIV

When you wonder if God is forgiving

The LORD is slow to anger and filled with
unfailing love, forgiving every kind of sin
and rebellion.

NUMBERS 14:18

Though we are overwhelmed by our sins,
   you forgive them all.

PSALM 65:3

The LORD is compassionate and merciful,
   slow to get angry and filled with unfailing
      love.
He will not constantly accuse us,
   nor remain angry forever.
He does not punish us for all our sins;
   he does not deal harshly with us, as we
      deserve.

PSALM 103:8-10

With the LORD there is unfailing love.
   His redemption overflows.

PSALM 130:7

The Lord our God is merciful and forgiving,
even though we have rebelled against him.

DANIEL 9:9

Jonah

> This change of plans greatly upset Jonah, and
> he became very angry. So he complained to the
> LORD about it: "Didn't I say before I left home
> that you would do this, LORD? That is why
> I ran away to Tarshish! I knew that you are a
> merciful and compassionate God, slow to get
> angry and filled with unfailing love. You are
> eager to turn back from destroying people."
>
> JONAH 4:1-2

The final chapter of the book of Jonah opens rather
curiously, but honestly. We're told that "this change
of plans greatly upset Jonah." For context, earlier,
the word of the Lord had come to Jonah with a clear
directive: "Get up and go to the great city of Nineveh.
Announce my judgment against it because I have seen
how wicked its people are."[5]

Rather than obeying God, Jonah ran the opposite
direction. His disobedience bred consequences—first,
for the sailors whose ship he had stowed away on, and
then for Jonah, as he was thrown overboard and swal-
lowed up by a great fish.

For three days and three nights, Jonah's heart was
softened by prayer, and eventually, the fish spit him

out. The Lord directed Jonah to Ninevah once again, but this time, Jonah obeyed. As Jonah preached, the people of Ninevah repented of their sins and came to follow God. The people's repentance "changed [God's] mind" about destroying their city.[6] Instead, he forgave and spared these once-wicked people.

This brings us back to Jonah 4. Notice that Jonah is upset. God's forgiveness seems unfair. And here we uncover why Jonah disobeyed in the first place: "Didn't I say before I left home that you would do this, LORD? That is why I ran away to Tarshish! I knew that you are a merciful and compassionate God, slow to get angry and filled with unfailing love. You are eager to turn back from destroying people."

Do you see it? The very same descriptors God uses in Exodus 34, Jonah uses here. In other words, God is acting true to his character. And that is good. But for us sinful, broken human beings, divine forgiveness often feels like a miscarriage of justice. This can be disorienting to the highest degree. This fact upsets Jonah so much that he wishes to die on the spot.[7]

Perhaps you feel the same. You can't understand how the person who hurt you could ever be forgiven for what they've done. Forgiveness feels like it will kill you.

And yet, notice God's response to Jonah: "Is it right for you to be angry about this?"[8] God is calling out Jonah's hypocrisy.

This question foreshadows Jesus' statement in his Sermon on the Mount: "God blesses those who are merciful, for they will be shown mercy."[9]

We can't give what we have not received. And we can't receive what we are not willing to give.

When you aren't sure why you need God's forgiveness

Everyone has sinned; we all fall short of
God's glorious standard.

ROMANS 3:23

The wages of sin is death, but the free gift of
God is eternal life through Christ Jesus our
Lord.

ROMANS 6:23

Temptation comes from our own desires,
which entice us and drag us away. These
desires give birth to sinful actions. And when
sin is allowed to grow, it gives birth to death.

JAMES 1:14-15

When you think that your sins are too great for God to ever forgive you

My friend, when you refuse to forgive yourself, you're not just hurting you. You're hurting God too! Failing to forgive ourselves eats at us in the worst way. We lose sight of our identity as slaves to Christ and instead become slaves to whatever it is that's holding us down and back. The sins of our past. The broken relationships. Our weaknesses. This doesn't have to be your story.

Our God is a God of forgiveness. This is who our God is. And our inability to see it doesn't change that fact; it only distorts God's character in our own minds. You. Are. Forgiven. Read that line over and over and over again.

These are not my words; these are God's words. God is beckoning you to return to him. His mercies are new every morning. "He has removed our sins as far from us as the east is from the west."[10] What a beautiful truth that is.

Forgive as the Lord forgave you.

COLOSSIANS 3:13, NIV

In him we have redemption through his blood, the forgiveness of sins, in accordance with the riches of God's grace.

EPHESIANS 1:7, NIV

All the prophets testify about him that everyone who believes in him receives forgiveness of sins through his name.

ACTS 10:43, NIV

Be merciful, just as your Father is merciful.

LUKE 6:36, NIV

The faithful love of the LORD never ends!
>His mercies never cease.
Great is his faithfulness;
>his mercies begin afresh each morning.

LAMENTATIONS 3:22-23

There is forgiveness of sins for all who repent.

LUKE 24:47

If we confess our sins to him, he is faithful
and just to forgive us our sins and to cleanse
us from all wickedness.

1 JOHN 1:9

**When you need to be reminded that God forgives your
sins through the death and resurrection of Jesus**

[Jesus] was pierced for our rebellion,
>crushed for our sins.
He was beaten so we could be whole.
>He was whipped so we could be healed.
All of us, like sheep, have strayed away.
>We have left God's paths to follow our own.
Yet the LORD laid on him
>the sins of us all.

ISAIAH 53:5-6

Because of Abraham's faith, God counted him
as righteous. And when God counted him as

righteous, it wasn't just for Abraham's benefit.
It was recorded for our benefit, too, assuring
us that God will also count us as righteous if
we believe in him, the one who raised Jesus
our Lord from the dead. He was handed over
to die because of our sins, and he was raised
to life to make us right with God.

ROMANS 4:22-25

Now we can rejoice in our wonderful new
relationship with God because our Lord
Jesus Christ has made us friends of God.

ROMANS 5:11

God was in Christ, reconciling the world
to himself, no longer counting people's sins
against them.

2 CORINTHIANS 5:19

For God in all his fullness
     was pleased to live in Christ,
and through him God reconciled
     everything to himself.
He made peace with everything in heaven and
          on earth
     by means of Christ's blood on the cross.

This includes you who were once far away
from God. You were his enemies, separated

from him by your evil thoughts and actions.
Yet now he has reconciled you to himself
through the death of Christ in his physical
body. As a result, he has brought you into
his own presence, and you are holy and
blameless as you stand before him without a
single fault.

COLOSSIANS 1:19-22

Just as each person is destined to die once and
after that comes judgment, so also Christ was
offered once for all time as a sacrifice to take
away the sins of many people.

HEBREWS 9:27-28

The Israelites in the Desert

Our ancestors were proud and stubborn, and
they paid no attention to your commands.
They refused to obey and did not remember
the miracles you had done for them. Instead,
they became stubborn and appointed a
leader to take them back to their slavery in
Egypt. But you are a God of forgiveness,
gracious and merciful, slow to become
angry, and rich in unfailing love. You did
not abandon them, even when they made an
idol shaped like a calf and said, "This is your

god who brought you out of Egypt!" They
committed terrible blasphemies.

But in your great mercy you did not
abandon them to die in the wilderness. The
pillar of cloud still led them forward by
day, and the pillar of fire showed them the
way through the night. You sent your good
Spirit to instruct them, and you did not stop
giving them manna from heaven or water
for their thirst. For forty years you sustained
them in the wilderness, and they lacked
nothing. Their clothes did not wear out, and
their feet did not swell!

NEHEMIAH 9:16-21

Choices have consequences—for better or worse.
Humans are not equal to God. Yet, in an attempt to
become like God, we consumed fruit from the tree of
life, which changed our relationship with him forever.[11]

God knew that his perfect nature had to be preserved. So, with sin came separation. God declared
that Adam and Eve must leave the place where heaven
and earth collided.

Death and de-creation would follow. From Adam
to his son Cain, from Cain to his son Lamech. From
Lamech to his son Nimrod. On and on it goes, as sin,
destruction, and death wreaked havoc on the world.

Eventually God allowed the chaos that humanity had entrenched itself in to run rampant. The floodwaters were released, and creation was swept away. The world was unmade.

But in God's kindness, a remnant was preserved. Noah, whose name is Comfort, took a role like Adam's. He ruled the animals who lived on his great ship, and when the waters receded, he found himself on a mountain, where he planted a garden.

Another chance. Then he fell too.

Sin and its subsequent master—death—still infected the world. Once again, God established a covenant—a promise to bring the snake crusher to bear through a particular family line of a particular nation. A promise to bring redemption and forgiveness. It started with a man named Abram, whose blessing would be passed on to his son Isaac. Isaac passed on the blessing to his son Jacob, who would be renamed Israel—the nation that would one day come. But in the midst of the promise, pain ensued. Deception and violence and sin continued to rule.

During this time, God seemingly retreated. For four hundred years, his absence was felt—until the covenant was revived and a nation was born.

It is here that we meet Moses, who appeared before Pharaoh and declared for the Lord, "Let my people go."[12] But Pharaoh refused. A hardened heart made solid stone by generations of sin, violence, and destruction that had ravaged the world.

Exodus, liberation, and freedom would not be given by the man they called god. So, the God of the universe stepped in. And de-creation reentered the picture . . .

In the wake of all that, a people—a faithful people—were spared. Those spared were released, and the "mixed multitude," as Exodus 12:38 (ESV) says, ventured off into the desert to become a new nation—God's nation.

But they, too, would fail.

On and on the cycle continued. God's people would fail, God would cast judgment, a prophet would intercede, the people would repent, God would relent.

God's character proved time and again to be one of forgiveness, reconciliation, and restoration. Despite the Israelites' waywardness, God was faithful to provide sustenance—literally manna from heaven. Mercy, mercy, mercy was extended, with justice in tow.

The same is true for you and me. Despite our waywardness, the invitation to repent, to turn around, to come back, is always available. And at the end of the road is a Father with his arms wide open ready to embrace you.

When you recognize that you need God's forgiveness

Help us, O God of our salvation!
>Help us for the glory of your name.
Save us and forgive our sins
>for the honor of your name.

PSALM 79:9

Seek the LORD while you can find him.
>Call on him now while he is near.
Let the wicked change their ways
>and banish the very thought of doing wrong.
Let them turn to the LORD that he may have
>mercy on them.
>Yes, turn to our God, for he will forgive
>generously.

ISAIAH 55:6-7

Bring your confessions, and return to the LORD.
>Say to him,
"Forgive all our sins and graciously receive us,
>so that we may offer you our praises."

HOSEA 14:2

That is why the LORD says,
>"Turn to me now, while there is time.
Give me your hearts.
>Come with fasting, weeping, and mourning.

Don't tear your clothing in your grief,
> but tear your hearts instead."
Return to the LORD your God,
> for he is merciful and compassionate,
slow to get angry and filled with unfailing love.
> He is eager to relent and not punish.

JOEL 2:12-13

When you are tempted to try to earn God's forgiveness

People are counted as righteous, not because
of their work, but because of their faith in
God who forgives sinners.

ROMANS 4:5

When we were utterly helpless, Christ
came at just the right time and died for us
sinners.

ROMANS 5:6

God's free gift leads to our being made right
with God, even though we are guilty of
many sins.

ROMANS 5:16

God saved you by his grace when you
believed. And you can't take credit for this; it
is a gift from God. Salvation is not a reward

for the good things we have done, so none of us can boast about it.

EPHESIANS 2:8-9

The Prodigal Son

I will go home to my father and say, "Father, I have sinned against both heaven and you, and I am no longer worthy of being called your son. Please take me on as a hired servant."

So he returned home to his father. And while he was still a long way off, his father saw him coming. Filled with love and compassion, he ran to his son, embraced him, and kissed him. His son said to him, "Father, I have sinned against both heaven and you, and I am no longer worthy of being called your son."

But his father said to the servants, "Quick! Bring the finest robe in the house and put it on him. Get a ring for his finger and sandals for his feet. And kill the calf we have been fattening. We must celebrate with a feast, for this son of mine was dead and has now returned to life. He was lost, but now he is found." So the party began.

LUKE 15:18-24

Rembrandt was a seventeenth-century Dutch painter, and he created one of my all-time favorite paintings: *The Return of the Prodigal Son.* It sits in my study, and I look at it every morning. If you're unfamiliar with that story, you can read it for yourself in Luke 15 this week.

But for our intents and purposes, I just want you to observe the imagery and how Rembrandt portrays the father figure (God). Looking at a picture of the painting online, what do you notice?

Do you notice that the father is blind? That he does not *see* the physical mess, the uncleanliness, the raggedness of his wayward son?

Do you notice the father's hands? His left hand is a masculine hand—pulling the son in as a loving, safe father, reminding the son that he is secure in his father's arms. His right hand is a feminine hand—consoling the son, reminding him that he is in tender, loving care.

Do you notice the father's facial expression? It is neither disgusted nor disappointed. There's grief for the pain his son has endured, relief that the son has returned, but overall, a calm, collected *presence.*

Love made known.

My friend, wherever you're at today in your spiritual journey, if God is anything less than this—tender, warm, inviting, safe, strong, secure—then I believe curiosity is our pathway to clarity in seeing God for who he really is. And prayer is the vehicle to grow in the intimacy Jesus longs to experience with us.

He is waiting for you to come to him. As you make your way home, he runs toward you, ready to adorn you with his lavish, undeserved grace.

When you ask God to forgive your sins

Each of you must repent of your sins and turn to God, and be baptized in the name of Jesus Christ for the forgiveness of your sins. Then you will receive the gift of the Holy Spirit. This promise is to you, to your children, and to those far away—all who have been called by the Lord our God.

ACTS 2:38-39

He is so rich in kindness and grace that he purchased our freedom with the blood of his Son and forgave our sins.

EPHESIANS 1:7

He has rescued us from the kingdom of darkness and transferred us into the Kingdom of his dear Son, who purchased our freedom and forgave our sins.

COLOSSIANS 1:13-14

You were dead because of your sins and
because your sinful nature was not yet cut
away. Then God made you alive with Christ,
for he forgave all our sins.

COLOSSIANS 2:13

It is by his great mercy that we have been
born again, because God raised Jesus
Christ from the dead. Now we live with
great expectation, and we have a priceless
inheritance—an inheritance that is kept in
heaven for you, pure and undefiled, beyond
the reach of change and decay. And through
your faith, God is protecting you by his
power until you receive this salvation, which
is ready to be revealed on the last day for all
to see.

1 PETER 1:3-5

When you need assurance that God has forgiven you

His unfailing love toward those who fear him
    is as great as the height of the heavens above
        the earth.
He has removed our sins as far from us
    as the east is from the west.

PSALM 103:11-12

I—yes, I alone—will blot out your sins for my
    own sake
  and will never think of them again.

ISAIAH 43:25

Just as sin ruled over all people and brought
them to death, now God's wonderful grace
rules instead, giving us right standing with
God and resulting in eternal life through
Jesus Christ our Lord.

ROMANS 5:21

Then he says,
    "I will never again remember
    their sins and lawless deeds."

HEBREWS 10:17

When you aren't sure how to respond to God's forgiveness

Let all that I am praise the LORD;
    may I never forget the good things he does
        for me.
He forgives all my sins
    and heals all my diseases.
He redeems me from death
    and crowns me with love and tender mercies.

PSALM 103:2-4

We praise God for the glorious grace he has poured out on us who belong to his dear Son.

EPHESIANS 1:6

Since we have a great High Priest who rules over God's house, let us go right into the presence of God with sincere hearts fully trusting him. For our guilty consciences have been sprinkled with Christ's blood to make us clean, and our bodies have been washed with pure water.

HEBREWS 10:21-22

Praise the LORD!
   Salvation and glory and power belong to our
      God.
His judgments are true and just.

REVELATION 19:1-2

Jesus Anointed by the Sinful Woman

One of the Pharisees asked Jesus to have dinner with him, so Jesus went to his home and sat down to eat. When a certain immoral woman from that city heard he was eating there, she brought a beautiful alabaster jar filled with expensive perfume. Then she knelt behind him at his feet, weeping. Her tears fell on his feet, and she wiped them off with her hair. Then she kept kissing his feet and putting perfume on them.

When the Pharisee who had invited him saw this, he said to himself, "If this man were a prophet, he would know what kind of woman is touching him. She's a sinner!"

Then Jesus answered his thoughts. "Simon," he said to the Pharisee, "I have something to say to you."

"Go ahead, Teacher," Simon replied.

Then Jesus told him this story: "A man loaned money to two people—500 pieces of silver to one and 50 pieces to the other. But neither of them could repay him, so he kindly forgave them both, canceling their debts. Who do you suppose loved him more after that?"

Simon answered, "I suppose the one for whom he canceled the larger debt."

"That's right," Jesus said. Then he turned to the woman and said to Simon, "Look at this woman kneeling here. When I entered your home, you didn't offer me water to wash the dust from my feet, but she has washed them with her tears and wiped them with her hair. You didn't greet me with a kiss, but from the time I first came in, she has not stopped kissing my feet. You neglected the courtesy of olive oil to anoint my head, but she has anointed my feet with rare perfume.

"I tell you, her sins—and they are many—have been forgiven, so she has shown me much love. But a person who is forgiven little shows only little love." Then Jesus said to the woman, "Your sins are forgiven."

The men at the table said among themselves, "Who is this man, that he goes around forgiving sins?"

And Jesus said to the woman, "Your faith has saved you; go in peace."

LUKE 7:36-50

When you truly understand what Jesus has done for you, there is no other response than worship. Simon—a Pharisee—could not understand why Jesus would ever let a woman like this near him. *She's a sinner!* he thought. And yet, notice how the text says, "Jesus answered his *thoughts*." Here we see Jesus' divine nature on full display. He has no patience for pretentiousness. Everyone is welcome at his feet. "Whoever wants to be my disciple must deny themselves and take up their cross and follow me."[13] Last I checked, whoever means whoever.

When we recognize the amount of grace that has been extended toward us, we have no room for judging others. "Do not judge, or you too will be judged. For in the same way you judge others, you will be judged, and with the measure you use, it will be measured to you," Jesus tells us.[14] Notice what Jesus is not saying. He's not saying to abandon all principle and conviction. He's not permitting us to live our lives any way we want. And he's not saying we should live without wisdom or awareness. Jesus isn't seeking to root out *integrity* under the guise of "no judgment." He's seeking to root out *idolatry*—the destructive mindset that elevates *our* rule over *God's* rule.

This Pharisee believed he was in the place of God. And then God himself corrected him.

Jesus' posture throughout his life and ministry is one of *release*, not *resentment*. It's one of *invitation*, not *intimidation*. The invitation is not to condemn others but to lovingly correct them only after we have been properly convicted and dealt with the sin in our own lives.

To Jesus, order matters.

When you need to be reminded that God promises future reconciliation and restoration for all people

There is a future coming where those who were once enemies are now friends, where strangers are neighbors, and where rivals are joined arm in arm. There is a future where we extend God's grace freely to others and live forgiven. If this is not the preferred future that we are working toward, then we must ask if the Savior who cast forgiveness down from the cross is the Savior we truly follow.

Forgiveness is required, but not everyone is obedient to Jesus' teaching. Jesus, in his kindness, has given us free will to choose. But to leave a legacy is not inevitable. We will be remembered by someone for our actions and behavior. We must decide if forgiveness will be included in our eulogy.

If it isn't, there is a price to pay. As the spiritual writer Henri Nouwen once said, "By not forgiving, I chain myself to a desire to get even, thereby losing my freedom. A forgiven person forgives. This is what we proclaim when we pray, 'and forgive us our trespasses as we forgive those who have trespassed against us.' This lifelong struggle lies at the heart of the Christian life."[15]

Could it be that you haven't fully embraced being forgiven? Could the bondage that has ensnared you throughout life be rooted in bitterness and resentment? Could your inability to forgive be holding you back from the freedom you long for? What if you could choose another way?

As the Catholic mystic Fr. Ron Rolheiser so beautifully penned,

> Before we die, we need to forgive. We need to forgive those who hurt us, to forgive ourselves for not being any better than those who hurt us, to forgive life itself for some of the things that it dealt us, and, not least, to forgive God for the fact that life is unfair, so as not to die with a bitter and angry heart. Gratitude is the fruit of that struggle.[16]

An invitation exists today to experience what is to come, though not quite in full. One day, Jesus will return and make all things new. There will be no more relational strife, pain, or hurt. All people will live in peace. Sin, death, and evil will be no more.

So, press on, my friend. That day is coming . . .

> The LORD will mediate between peoples
> and will settle disputes between strong
> nations far away.
> They will hammer their swords into plowshares
> and their spears into pruning hooks.
> Nation will no longer fight against nation,
> nor train for war anymore.

Everyone will live in peace and prosperity,
    enjoying their own grapevines and fig trees,
    for there will be nothing to fear.
The Lord of Heaven's Armies
    has made this promise!

MICAH 4:3-4

This is the new covenant I will make
    with the people of Israel on that day, says the
        Lord:
I will put my laws in their minds,
    and I will write them on their hearts.
I will be their God,
    and they will be my people.
And they will not need to teach their neighbors,
    nor will they need to teach their relatives,
    saying, "You should know the Lord."
For everyone, from the least to the greatest,
    will know me already.
And I will forgive their wickedness,
    and I will never again remember their sins.

HEBREWS 8:10-12

I heard a loud shout from the throne,
saying, "Look, God's home is now among
his people! He will live with them, and they
will be his people. God himself will be with
them. He will wipe every tear from their

eyes, and there will be no more death or
sorrow or crying or pain. All these things are
gone forever."

———

With that, our time together has concluded, though I suspect this will not be the last time we interact. In fact, I'd encourage you to please not make this a one-stop read. My hunch is that although you've finished this book, your journey of forgiveness has just begun.

We have walked through Scripture—both Old and New Testament—and have witnessed, firsthand, how imperative forgiveness and reconciliation are when it comes to life in the Kingdom of God.

But as I said at the beginning, the journey of forgiveness often goes one of two ways: Either the fire of relational strife and conflict rages out of control and burns everyone involved. Or . . . the fire of forgiveness becomes a crucible that refines us into people of love, joy, peace, patience, and kindness.

I hope that by this point, you're longing for the latter. But it's not easy. It's simple, but it's not easy.

And so, perhaps you will need to return to this book and try again and again . . . and again. My suspicion is that if this is your process, you're probably on the right track. Because forgiveness is rarely linear. There's no formula, simply a fire. Two steps forward, three steps back.

As long as you're taking steps, you're at least moving more toward holiness than bitterness. And that is where I'd like to leave you—with taking steps. Perhaps today you need to

- send a text
- make a call
- write a letter
- meet up for coffee
- ask for forgiveness
- receive forgiveness

All of this is the foundation for becoming practitioners of forgiveness. Forgiveness cannot remain an ideal or a theory; it must be worked out in the real situations of day-to-day life.

Day after day, over time, this helps to secure our forgiving future. A future where ultimate reconciliation takes place. Where relationships are restored, lives are healed, and life is found. This future is for everyone, yes, everyone who repents and believes in the Good News of Jesus Christ. His transformative power is available to us now—if we only ask for what we've already received.

Verses on Forgiveness

I have found that, on particular days, being able to locate what God's Word says about forgiveness is extremely helpful and comforting. And so, I've taken time to compile what the Bible has to say regarding forgiveness in the order that the verses occur canonically. I hope and pray they bring peace and hope to your soul in times of need.

Genesis 50:17	Psalm 25:11
Exodus 10:17	Psalm 32:5
Exodus 23:21	Psalm 65:3
Exodus 32:32	Psalm 79:9
Exodus 34:9	Psalm 86:5
Numbers 14:19	Psalm 103:10-14
1 Samuel 15:25	Psalm 130:4
1 Kings 8:30	Proverbs 28:13
1 Kings 8:50	Isaiah 1:18
2 Chronicles 6:21	Isaiah 53:5
2 Chronicles 7:14	Isaiah 55:7
Psalm 19:12	Jeremiah 5:7

Jeremiah 31:34	Acts 2:38
Jeremiah 33:8	Acts 3:19
Jeremiah 50:20	Acts 5:31
Daniel 9:19	Acts 10:43
Hosea 14:2	Romans 8:1
Micah 7:18-19	Romans 12:18
Matthew 5:23-24	Romans 12:14, 15-17, 19
Matthew 6:9-15	2 Corinthians 2:5-11
Matthew 18:15-18	2 Corinthians 5:18, 20
Matthew 18:21-22	Ephesians 1:7
Matthew 18:35	Ephesians 4:31-32
Matthew 26:28	Colossians 1:13-14
Mark 2:10	Colossians 3:13
Mark 11:25	2 Timothy 3:1-5
Luke 5:24	Hebrews 8:12
Luke 6:37	Hebrews 10:17
Luke 11:4	Hebrews 12:14-15
Luke 17:3-4	1 Peter 2:21
Luke 19:8	1 Peter 2:23
Luke 23:34	1 John 1:9
John 17:20-23	1 John 2:1
John 20:23	1 John 2:3, 6, 9-10

Notes

INTRODUCTION

1. Some people also define forgiveness as "to stop being angry about a wrong thing someone has done to you and to forget about it." However, I fundamentally disagree with this definition, as I argue extensively throughout my book *Three Strikes, You're Forgiven.*
2. Genesis 16:13.
3. Matthew 6:14-15.

FORGIVING OTHERS

1. Luke 23:34.
2. James 2:12-13, NIV.
3. 1 Peter 2:23.
4. Trisha Winter, "Forgive as Jesus Forgives," Centralia Community Church, March 28, 2021, https://cccog.com /beyond-sunday/2021/3/29/forgive-as-jesus-forgives.
5. "Matthew 18—Qualities and Attitudes of Kingdom Citizens," Enduring Word, accessed December 16, 2024, https://enduringword.com/bible-commentary/matthew-18/.
6. Matthew 18:28-30.
7. Martin Luther King Jr., "Loving Your Enemies" in *Strength to Love* (Fortess Press, 1981), 51.

8. Matthew 5:23-24, NIV.

9. Luke 23:34, NIV.

10. 2 Corinthians 12:7.

11. Romans 3:23.

12. Bessel A. van der Kolk, *The Body Keeps the Score* (Penguin Books, 2015).

13. Ron Bruner, "Becoming a Better Parent: The Five Dimensions of Trauma," Westview Boys' Home, March 24, 2024, https://westviewboyshome.com/becoming-a-better -parent-the-five-dimensions-of-trauma/.

14. 2 Corinthians 2:8.

ASKING FOR FORGIVENESS

1. Blue Letter Bible, "metanoeō (*v.*)," accessed November 7, 2024, https://www.blueletterbible.org/lexicon/g3340/kjv /tr/0-1/.

2. Galatians 6:7, NIV; Habakkuk 1:13, NIV.

3. Romans 2:4.

4. Hebrews 10:19-22.

5. Jennie Allen, "The War for Your Faith with John Mark Comer," *Made for This*, October 21, 2021, https://www .jennieallen.com/blog/the-war-for-your-faith-with-john -mark-comer.

6. 2 Samuel 11:1-5.

7. 2 Samuel 11:6-13.

8. 2 Samuel 11:14-27.

9. John 8:3-4, NIV.

10. Bible Hub, s.v. "histémi (*v.*)," accessed November 6, 2024, https://biblehub.com/greek/2476.htm.

11. Genesis 33:4.

12. Genesis 33:2-3, NIV.

FORGIVING YOURSELF

1. 1 John 1:9, NIV.

2. Romans 7:15, NIV.

3. John 20:19, 21, 26.

4. John 21:19, NIV.

FORGIVING GOD

1. Justin Taylor, "Tozer vs. Lewis: What's the Most Important Thing About Us?," *The Gospel Coalition* (blog), June 4, 2016, https://www.thegospelcoalition.org/blogs/justin -taylor/tozer-vs-lewis-whats-the-most-important-thing-about -us/.

2. Exodus 34:6-7, NIV.

3. 1 John 4:19, NIV.

4. John 3:16-17, NIV.

5. Jonah 1:2.

6. Jonah 3:10.

7. Jonah 4:3.

8. Jonah 4:4.

9. Matthew 5:7.

10. Psalm 103:12.

11. The content in this paragraph and the following has been summarized and adapted from Blaine Eldredge, *The Paradise King: The Tragic History and Spectacular Future of Everything According to Jesus of Nazareth* (Iona Farms Books, 2023).

12. Exodus 5:1.

13. Matthew 16:24, NIV.

14. Matthew 7:1-2, NIV.

15. Henri J. M. Nouwen, *The Road to Daybreak: A Spiritual Journey* (Image Books, 1990), 68.

16. Ron Rolheiser, Facebook, April 6, 2022, https://www .facebook.com/ronrolheiser/posts/before-we-die-we-need-to -forgive-we-need-to-forgive-those-who-hurt-us-to-forgive /4974782953656517/.

About the Author

MICAH E. DAVIS lives and writes inside "the loop" of Indianapolis, Indiana, with his wife, Rylei, and their Australian kelpie, Leo. He is the pastor of teaching and vision at The Sanctuary: a church in the neighborhood, for the city. The Sanctuary's mission is to be and become a haven for broken people to practice the way of Jesus, participate in community, and permeate the world.

Before cofounding The Sanctuary, Micah was a high school pastor at a suburban megachurch on the north side of Indianapolis. Micah has a Bachelor of Science in liberal arts from Indiana Wesleyan University (2019) and became an ordained minister in 2021.

He is the author of *Trailblazers: A Journey to Discover God's Purpose for Your Life* and *Three Strikes, You're Forgiven: Encounter a God Who Wants to Redeem Your Past, Restore Your Present, and Transform Your Future.*

Micah believes the written and spoken word are mediums to elicit heart change and life transformation. He has committed his life to using words for *good*.

For more of Micah's teachings on faith, formation, and the life of Jesus, go to sanctuaryindy.com and sign up for the podcast, or visit micahedavis.com.

What Next?

Good books deserve to be shared.

If you've found this work helpful, it would mean the world to me if you'd consider

- posting a review at your favorite online bookseller;
- posting a picture on social media about why you enjoyed the book;
- sending a note to a friend who you think would benefit from this work. Or, even better, gifting them a copy yourself.

After a good read, I'm always looking for more. If it's helpful to you, below is a QR code to access more of my teachings and writings on faith, formation, and the life of Jesus.

You can also learn more at sanctuaryindy.com or by visiting micahedavis.com.

May the peace of Christ be upon you,

ALSO AVAILABLE FROM MICAH E. DAVIS AND TYNDALE HOUSE PUBLISHERS

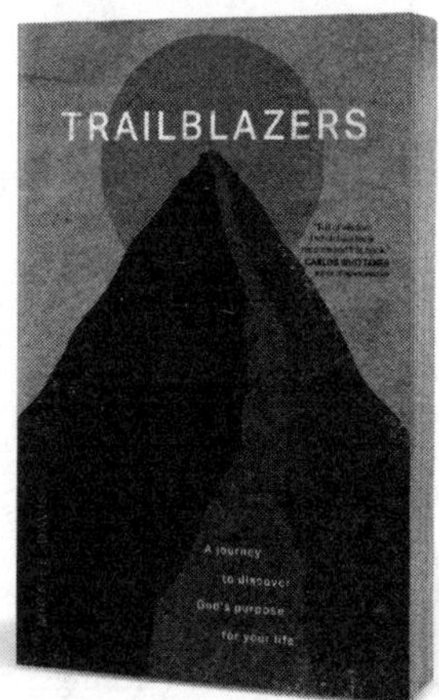

We all want our lives to count for something. In *Trailblazers*, using biblical characters and his own life experiences, Micah shows how a life that is built on a solid foundation of faith can lead us to blaze a new trail . . . a unique one God has purposed only for us.

In *Three Strikes, You're Forgiven*, we are invited to let go of our restless pursuit of perfection and to find rest in Christ.

Available everywhere books are sold.

Accompanying video streaming sessions available at tyndalechristianresources.com.

CP2050